W9-AHY-786

J
599.32
Fis
Fischer-Nagel
Inside the burrow

398060
12.95

DATE DUE			

Rb

✓

GREAT RIVER REGIONAL LIBRARY

St. Cloud, Minnesota 56301

Inside the Burrow

The Life of the Golden Hamster

Inside the Burrow
The Life of the Golden Hamster

by Heiderose and Andreas Fischer-Nagel

A Carolrhoda Nature Watch Book

Carolrhoda Books, Inc./Minneapolis

223 7329

Thanks to Erik Heikkila, Veterinary Technician, PETCETERA, Richfield, Minnesota, for his assistance with this book

This edition first published 1986 by Carolrhoda Books, Inc.
Original edition published 1984 by Kinderbuchverlag KBV Luzern AG,
Lucerne, Switzerland, under the title IM HAMSTERBAU
Copyright © 1984 Kinderbuchverlag KBV Luzern AG
Translation from the German © 1985 by J.M. Dent & Sons Ltd.
Adapted by Carolrhoda Books, Inc.
All rights reserved.

Manufactured in the United States of America

This book is available in two editions:
Library binding by Carolrhoda Books, Inc.
Soft cover by First Avenue Editions
241 First Avenue North
Minneapolis, Minnesota 55401

LIBRARY OF CONGRESS CATALOGING-IN-PUBLICATION DATA

Fischer-Nagel, Heiderose.
　　Inside the burrow.

　　"A Carolrhoda nature watch book."
　　Translation of: Im Hamsterbau.
　　Summary: Describes the characteristics and
behavior of hamsters both in the wild and in captivity,
as demonstrated by a pair observed in a burrow built
by the authors. Includes information on caring for
pet hamsters.
　　1. Hamsters—Juvenile literature. 2. Hamsters as
pets—Juvenile literature. [1. Hamsters]
I. Fischer-Nagel, Andreas. II. Title.
QL737.R638F5313　1986　　599.32'33　　86-2591
ISBN 0-87614-286-2 (lib. bdg.)
ISBN 0-87614-478-4 (pbk.)

2　3　4　5　6　7　8　9　10　96　95　94　93　92　91　90　89　88　87

For our children
Tamarica and Cosmea Désirée

398060

Hamsters are tiny animals that have become very popular house pets. The most popular **species**, or kind, is the golden hamster, which is about 6 inches (about 15 cm) long and weighs about 2.8 ounces (about 80 g). The golden hamster was first discovered in Syria in 1839. However, it was not until 1930 that a scientist captured a mother golden and her young and brought them into his laboratory to see if he could raise them in captivity. Although not all of these survived, every golden hamster living today is descended from the litter found just over 50 years ago.

Hamsters are members of the scientific order of **rodents**, which also includes rats, mice, squirrels, beavers, and many other mammals. Like other rodents, hamsters are **burrowing** animals, which means they dig underground tunnels, or burrows, in which to live.

Hamsters have a strong instinct to **hoard** their food. They constantly gather large amounts of food and hide it away in the burrow. In fact, the word hamster comes from the German word *hamstern*, which means "to hoard."

Hamsters are **nocturnal** animals, which means they are active mostly at night. During the day, they curl up in their burrows and sleep. They do not like being disturbed during the day and will attack any animal or person that tries to wake them up before they're ready to be woken. When the sun goes down, they wake up and begin their hunting and digging.

Life for caged golden hamsters is, of course, different from their life in the wild. In this book, we will see two golden hamsters that have been removed from their cages and placed in a homemade burrow. These hamsters will show what life is like for the kinds of hamsters still found in the wild, and how some of these wild behaviors are present in pet hamsters, too.

Hamsters spend most of their lives underground in their burrows. Each hamster digs its own burrow, so no two are exactly alike. Each burrow has a long entrance tunnel and sometimes one or more other entrances as well. There are several different "rooms" in each burrow: a sleeping chamber, store-rooms for food, and even a "bathroom."

The passageways are just large enough for the hamster to fit through. They are so narrow that it is surprising the animal does not get stuck! But the hamsters can move very quickly as they thread their way back and forth bringing in food to be stored for the winter.

Wild hamsters **hibernate** during the winter. When an animal hibernates, its bodily functions slow down drastically, and it goes into a deep sleep. When a hamster hibernates, its heart rate slows from about 400 to just 4 beats per minute. Hibernating hamsters usually wake up about once a week to eat some of the food they have stored away. Then they continue their hibernation. Hamsters kept as pets will hibernate, too, if the room they are kept in becomes cooler than 45 degrees F (7 degrees C).

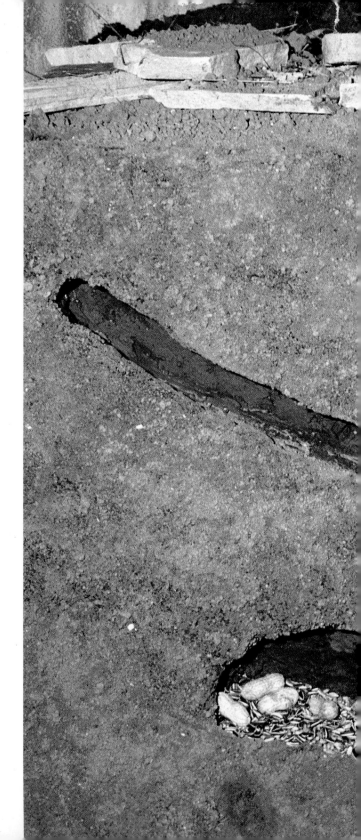

The hamster's instinct to burrow is extremely strong, so it is not surprising that hamsters are expert burrow-diggers. A hamster's sharp-clawed paws are perfect digging tools. With its front paws, it scrapes the soil beneath its belly. Then, when a small mound has accumulated, the hamster brings the hind legs forward and uses them to push the soil backwards. This is repeated as long as the hamster feels any loose soil beneath it. It then continues digging with its forepaws. It is amazing that such tiny, delicate paws, which look a lot like miniature human hands, can dig through hard soil so easily. The hamster's hind leg muscles are very strong, too, and enable the animal to crawl both forward and backward in the tunnel.

In his food storage chamber, a hamster hoards many different kinds of fruit and seeds as well as herbs, grasses, grains, nuts, and vegetables. A wild hamster will also occasionally eat insects or even a tiny fieldmouse.

Hamsters collect food by cramming it into their cheek pouches, carrying it back to the burrow, then spitting it out again. Hamsters unload their cheek pouches by pushing on their full cheeks with their front paws.

Storage compartments are large and often contain more than 2 pounds (1 kg) of grain. Even when the hamster has plenty of food, it instinctively keeps hoarding more and more.

Hamsters are extremely clean animals. They never dirty their nests and are careful always to use their "bathroom" chamber. When this chamber is full, it is blocked off with earth, and a fresh one is dug.

Sometimes the hamster's snout gets dirty or wet. When that happens, it immediately washes and dries its face with its forepaws until it is clean again. Hamsters track down food with their noses, and their sensitive whiskers are used to test the size of the holes in their burrows.

A hamster's **incisor** (in-SIZE-er), or gnawing teeth, are sharp enough to gnaw through cardboard or wood. Like all rodents, a hamster has four incisors, two in the upper jaw and two in the lower. They are visible at birth and grow continuously. Because the incisors keep growing, a hamster must gnaw constantly in order to wear them down. If the hamster had nothing to gnaw on, its incisors would eventually grow so long that the hamster could not close its mouth or chew. It would probably starve to death.

In the wild, hamsters have many enemies, such as foxes, wolves, hawks, and eagles. When threatened by such an animal, a hamster's first impulse is to escape by hiding in its burrow. If that isn't possible, it uses its sharp teeth to defend itself. If caught by surprise, the hamster rolls quickly onto its back and bares its teeth. Any animal coming too close will be pushed away vigorously with the feet and given a sharp bite. A hamster bite can leave a nasty wound.

As soon as the weather gets warmer and hamsters wake from their hibernation, they mate. Tame ones mate throughout the year. In this photo, the male hamster is looking for a female to mate with. Using scent that he secretes from a special gland on the side of his body, he marks different parts of the female's **territory**, or area where she lives. By doing this he claims her as his mate.

Hamsters are loners by nature. So when they do meet, they act very cautiously at first. Unless the female is ready to mate, which happens about every fourth day for the first year of her life, she will have nothing to do with the male and will chase him away. Female hamsters are almost always more aggressive than males.

When she is ready to mate, the female crouches on the ground while the male mounts her from the back and deposits his **sperm**, or male reproductive cells, into her. During mating, the male often grasps the loose skin of the female's neck in his teeth.

After mating, the male and female remain together peacefully for a few days. The female then becomes increasingly nervous and aggressive until she finally chases away the male. If left together, she would probably kill him.

About one week later, the female starts getting ready for the birth of her young. She works hard at collecting soft nesting material, such as moss, hay, dry leaves, and animal fur, with which to prepare a nest. If any of the nesting material she has gathered is too coarse or hard, she gnaws it until it is soft enough to suit her.

Female golden hamsters can give birth

up to six times a year. The size of the **litter**, or group of babies, generally varies between four and twelve, but it is sometimes larger. Golden hamsters have a **gestation period**, or time between mating and birth, that is very short, just sixteen days.

In the photograph below, you can see how the female squats on her hind legs for the birth, her head bent forward. This position is quite different from that of dogs and cats, which usually either lie on their sides or remain standing when giving birth.

Each birth takes place so quickly that it is usually impossible to see what is happening. The moment a baby appears the mother begins licking it to clean it and to release it from the thin transparent sac that surrounds the baby before birth. The mother then bites through the **umbilical cord,** through which the baby received food and oxygen while inside its mother, and then eats the cord and the sac.

Hamsters are born blind and completely helpless. At birth they are less than 1 inch (2 or 3 cm) long and weigh less than a quarter of an ounce (7 or 8 g). They have no fur when born but are pink and hairless. In the few minutes before the second baby is born, the first finds one of its mother's nipples and starts to **suckle,** or drink her milk.

If a mother hamster with young babies is disturbed, she will carry her young to safety in some other part of her burrow. She either "swallows" them into her cheek pouches or grasps them with her teeth. While they are being carried, the young remain absolutely relaxed and still so they are not hurt by their mother's sharp teeth.

The sound of the babies drinking, along with their tiny squeaks, can soon be heard again from the new nesting spot, where the babies and their mother are safe and cozy.

When the babies are tiny, the hamster mother sits over her litter like a hen on her eggs. She covers them so carefully that they are almost hidden from sight. The babies grow bigger by the day. They also begin growing soft fur coats. Young hamsters spend a great deal of time napping in the nest, snuggled together for warmth and protection.

When the babies are about a week old, they are still being nursed by their mother. But they are also beginning to search for solid food to eat. They soon learn how to grasp nuts in their tiny paws and to nibble them with their sharp teeth. Once they have eaten, they clean themselves carefully. They wipe their snouts with their front paws until the last crumb of food is gone.

The mother hamster works hard to keep herself and her babies well fed. She searches for food, stuffing as much as she can into her cheeks. She puts small, edible pieces straight into her mouth. Anything larger she first holds in her paws and gnaws into smaller bits before transferring it to her cheek pouches.

At two weeks of age, the hamster babies' eyes open. By three weeks, they are extremely active. They enjoy running up and down the passageways, exploring every part of the burrow. Even at this young age, the hamsters spend a lot of time and energy moving food from one hiding place to another. This hoarding and hiding of food is such a strong instinct, even pet hamsters do it.

The growing hamsters go through many changes. Each day they dash more and more energetically through the burrow, trampling the nest flat as they go. They start learning to use the bathroom chamber (picture above left), which greatly helps to keep the nest clean. They explore the burrow's various compartments, play or fight with one another, and romp in the passageways. The older they get, the braver they are about exploring their surroundings.

The babies' fur begins growing about two weeks after birth. Soon it is as thick and silky-soft as that of the adult animals. Golden hamsters' coats are a rich golden-brown color on the upper parts and off-white underneath. Their necks are tinged with black. The **guard hairs**, or long, coarse hairs protecting the soft fur underneath, appear to be completely brown. But if you blow gently into the coat you will see that the individual hairs are mostly gray. Only the tips are brown.

As the young hamsters become bolder, they discover how to get out of their burrow. One after another they stick their heads out of the entrance hole. Peering and sniffing all around, they carefully climb into the open and explore their surroundings. Every new discovery has to be thoroughly examined.

The hamsters quickly lose their fear of the outside world, and soon they are dashing in and out of the burrow. In fact, they are so anxious to explore that they push, shove, and trample each other as they try to get out.

As they explore farther away from the burrow, the young hamsters discover a variety of things to eat, such as seeds, leaves, roots, insects, or grains of wheat. Each hamster tries to find a tidbit of food to put into its cheek pouches and keep for itself. Usually, though, it has to fight its other litter mates for it as each tries to grab the food for itself.

In the right-hand photograph, four young hamsters have found a carrot half buried in the ground. Each one tries to bite off the largest piece either to swallow or to cram into its cheek pouches before the others get it all. The hamsters squeak with anger while they fight for the food.

The small hamsters grow very quickly. At four weeks they are already completely independent of their mother. At six weeks they are so well developed that it is better to separate them from one another as well as from their mother. When young hamsters in the wild cannot live together peacefully any longer, it is time for them to move away, dig their own burrows, pair off, and set about giving birth to a new generation.

Golden hamsters kept as pets need a strong wire cage with plenty of room to run and climb. It is best to have a cage that can be cleaned easily. Even though hamsters are very clean animals and will only use one corner of the cage as a "bathroom," you must clean the cage at least once a week. Wood shavings make good ground litter. For a nest, a hamster likes hay, straw, or dry sawdust. Your pet should also be given a few paper tissues that it can chew to make a soft bed. A water bottle like the one in the picture is very important. It keeps the water fresh at all times, and the hamster can drink just the amount it wants. Even though hamsters need water to drink, it is important to keep their cages dry. A hamster can get sick and even die from living in a wet cage.

Hamsters should be fed in the evening when they wake up. They should be given a mixture of cereals, which are available at pet shops, along with fresh raw fruits and vegetables. They also like a little chopped meat from time to time. Hamsters need lots of exercise to stay healthy, so get an exercise wheel for them to play on.

You can get excellent, detailed information on hamster care from breeders or pet shops. If you take good care of your hamster, it should live for two or three years, which is a hamster's normal lifespan. And if it lives as long as three years, you can be sure that you have looked after it very well.

In addition to the golden hamster, there are several other hamster species. These hamsters are all related, but they are somewhat different in size, shape, color, and behavior. The common or European hamster (above left) is the largest, the size of a guinea pig. The gray hamster and the dwarf hamster are two other types found in the wild. And breeders have introduced other varieties, such as the long-haired teddy bear hamster (below left) and many colorful short-haired hamsters (below), which make excellent and very attractive pets.

Both in the wild and in a cage, hamsters are lively, industrious animals. They are attractive and great fun. But hamsters are not only fine pets. They are very helpful to humans in more important ways. Hamsters are used by scientists as laboratory animals in experiments to help discover cures for diseases. Hamsters bring people pleasure, but the tiny creatures may also be helping to save lives.

GLOSSARY

burrow: to dig a tunnel; also, an underground tunnel or chamber

gestation period: the time between mating and birth, during which the young develop

guard hairs: long, coarse hairs that protect the softer fur underneath

hibernate: to pass the winter in an inactive state. During hibernation, all body functions slow down.

hoard: to store large amounts of something

incisor: large gnawing teeth

litter: the group of babies born at one time

nocturnal: active mostly at night

rodent: the scientific order of gnawing mammals that includes hamsters

species: a group of plants or animals that share similar characteristics

sperm: male reproductive cells

suckle: to drink the mother's milk

territory: the area in which an animal lives and claims as its own

umbilical cord: the cord that carries oxygen and nutrients to the developing young inside the mother's body before birth

ABOUT THE AUTHORS

Heiderose and Andreas Fischer-Nagel received degrees in biology from the University of Berlin. Their special interests include animal behavior, wildlife protection, and environmental control. The Fischer-Nagels have collaborated on several internationally successful science books for children. They attribute the success of their books to their "love of children and of our threatened environment" and believe that "children learning to respect nature today are tomorrow's protectors of nature."

The Fischer-Nagels live in Germany with their daughters, Tamarica and Cosmea Désirée.